The Gospel
According to Judas

by

KEITH HOLYOAK

DOS MADRES

2015

DOS MADRES PRESS INC.
P.O.Box 294, Loveland, Ohio 45140
www.dosmadres.com   editor@dosmadres.com

Dos Madres is dedicated to the belief that the small press is essential to the vitality of contemporary literature as a carrier of the new voice, as well as the older, sometimes forgotten voices of the past. And in an ever more virtual world, to the creation of fine books pleasing to the eye and hand.

Dos Madres is named in honor of Vera Murphy and Libbie Hughes, the "Dos Madres" whose contributions have made this press possible.

Dos Madres Press, Inc. is an Ohio Not For Profit Corporation and a 501 (c) (3) qualified public charity. Contributions are tax deductible.

Executive Editor: Robert J. Murphy

Illustration & Book Design: Elizabeth H. Murphy
www.illusionstudios.net

Cover art by Jim Holyoak

Typset in Adobe Garamond Pro & Sonyanna Script
ISBN 978-1-939929-30-3
Library of Congress Control Number: 2015932554

First Edition

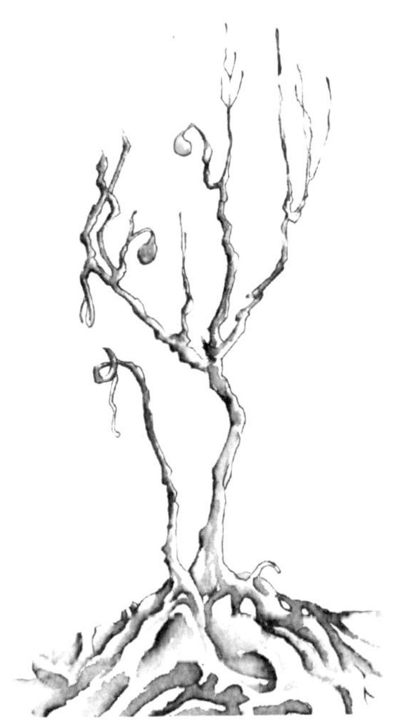

Jesus said, "Be passersby."

—*The Gospel of Thomas*

Every poem an epitaph.

—T. S. Eliot, "Little Gidding"

Table of Contents

Executor's Preface 1

Chapter 1. Double Cross...9

Chapter 2. Lamentation...10

Chapter 3. Samsara...11

Chapter 4. Invocation of Names....12

Chapter 5. Word....13

Chapter 6. Seed 14

Chapter 7. Return of the Fisher King....15

Chapter 8. Top Ten of Infamy.....16

Chapter 9. Genesis 17

Chapter 10. Beatitudes....20

Chapter 11. A Sea Crossing.....21

Chapter 12. Go!....25

Chapter 13. Songs of Mariam Magdala: Wisdom.....26

Chapter 14. Songs of Mariam Magdala: Lovesick.....27

Chapter 15. Songs of Mariam Magdala: Healing.......28

Chapter 16. Songs of Mariam Magdala: Love....29

Chapter 17. Ocean....30

Chapter 18. The Road Home.....31

Chapter 19. The Golden Gate.....34

Chapter 20. Climbing Mount Zion......35

Chapter 21. On the Fig Tree......40

Chapter 22. Coulda Binna Buddha.....41

Chapter 23. Judas Unmasked.......43

Chapter 24. The Ruined Temple 44

Chapter 25. Angkor Thom 45

Chapter 26. Dialogue of Judas and Jesus.....48

Chapter 27. Benediction.....50

Executor's Notes............. 51

About the Author............. 59

In accord with the author's wishes, I am now making this extraordinary document that has come into my possession available to the world. What it means is for each reader to judge. I, of course, have had my own reactions. But being neither author nor editor, but just the executor fulfilling an obligation that has been laid upon me, I will stand aside and let the author speak directly to you. Nonetheless, a little background regarding the provenance of the document may be of interest.

Much of the history is already widely known. Sometime in the 1970s, peasants in Egypt discovered a papyrus book that has since come to be known as the Tchacos Codex, dating from the third or fourth century. Extracted from a limestone box hidden in a burial cave, it passed through the hands of a series of shady dealers—languishing for seventeen years in a humid safe-deposit box in New York, at one point frozen, various pages torn and lost. By 2001 the book had come into the possession of Frieda Nussberger-Tchacos, an antiquities dealer. Concerned by its visible deterioration, she entrusted this treasure to reliable conservators and philologists. In 2006, the National Geographic Society published the first English translation of a Coptic text included in the Tchacos Codex— *The Gospel of Judas.*

The discovery after almost two millennia of a gospel written from the perspective of Judas Iscariot—the most reviled figure in the history of Christianity—was an astounding revelation. At first, many thought that *The Gospel of Judas* might finally solve the mystery of that primal crime (if crime it was)—the betrayal of Jesus by one of his chosen apostles. But the devil loves neither light nor dark, but rather delights in a twilight of dust and confusion. The lost lines and pages, the inevitable ambiguities that arise in translating from an extinct language, and the esoteric nature of the Gnostic version of Christianity reflected in the text, all conspired to fuel new controversies that simply added to the old ones. In any case, the text turned out to be (at best) a translation of a Greek manuscript from the early second century. Judas was the hero of *The Gospel of Judas,* but not its author.

My own small role in this matter was first signaled in the spring of 2007, when I unexpectedly received an email addressed from iscariotj@mail.com. Under the subject line of "Second Coming", I read in the body of the text:

I am back. Twenty centuries of stony sleep have been vexed to nightmare. My time is short, the darkness drops again. I need you to help me. Please reply.

My first reaction was that my spam filter had failed yet again, and that some crackpot was broadcasting delusional nonsense. The choice of email address seemed indicative of the sender's disturbed mental condition (or else of an odd sense of humor). Still, I was struck by the obvious allusions to William Butler Yeats, my favorite poet. Needless to say, I am hardly unique in my high regard for Yeats, so this was a flimsy basis for risking any intimacy with an anonymous stranger. Yet I could not help but feel some urge to connect with my fellow admirer of the Irish master. I was not so naïve as to succumb to this trap, of course, so after due reflection I made no reply. I did mention the odd communication to several friends over the next few days, to check whether a novel spoofing attack might be flooding inboxes with junk. However, no one I spoke with was aware of similar emails.

A week later I received the second message, which read:

Surely some revelation is at hand; surely the Second Coming is at hand. Someone must speak for the slouching beast. Please reply.

Disconcerted by the apocalyptic tone (the words again taken from the poet I admired), I still did not reply. The very next day a third message arrived:

The slouching sphinx will creep yet closer while it gauges when to make its final leap. You claim to speak for seers who die scapegoats—now speak for me. Please reply.

I must confess I was astounded. This time the allusion was apparently to my own poem "Girasol", which in 2005 had appeared in *Flaming Arrows,* an obscure literary magazine published in Ireland. (In 2010 the poem would be included in *My Minotaur,* a collection of my early poems.) I had no illusions about the size of my readership—the number of people who had read my poem at the time likely could be counted on the fingers of two hands (perhaps just one!). This time, despite the unsettling tone, my curiosity bested my commonsense. I clicked "reply".

One might say (to steal a line from Bogart) that this was the beginning of a beautiful friendship. For the next few years, from time to time with no clear pattern, he sent me bits and pieces of his writings. On occasion his messages would arrive in fevered bursts within a single day or overnight; other times they were separated by gaps that might stretch to months. Ours was an odd friendship to be sure—one-sided electronic transmissions of fragments of a manuscript, composed by someone supposedly dead for two millennia and mourned by no one. Yet still, the mere fact that Judas had selected me to do his bidding—to put together his *Gospel* and make it public—could not help but create, if not genuine friendship, then at least sympathy for the devil. His final message to me (over a year ago now) was simply, "It is finished. Make my words known in your time." I have not heard from him since.

I have often wondered, of course, why Judas picked me for his task. He never explained. His writing focuses on those great events of long ago, not the personal circumstances of his own second coming (though he is evidently aware of at least some of what transpired during his long absence). Maybe some shared poetic instinct played a role. I recall that decades ago, when I was a boy growing up on a farm in British Columbia, I endeavored to translate the canonical gospel story into verse. Judas, in creating his own *Gospel,* was clearly at great pains to speak as a poet, even while working in a language so new to him. Those earliest messages, before he began to entrust his actual text to me, attest to a poetic connection.

But perhaps there was more to it than that. As time went on, I grew suspicious that something personal connected the two of us. In his later writings Judas started to reveal knowledge about me that seemed strikingly direct. It occurred to me that he might be a stalker, somehow participating in my everyday life yet invisible to me. As you can imagine, this possibility was quite disconcerting. I began to scrutinize my closest friends, wondering if someone near and dear to me was a reborn Judas. Could it be that his *Gospel* was actually being sent to me as some sort of warning, that some new betrayal was being plotted?

My hyper-vigilance began to interfere with my everyday life. Both at home and work I checked my email incessantly, as if the next missive from Judas might finally clear up a mystery that now oppressed me. Fortunately I was due for a sabbatical (I am a university professor). In Los Angeles, where I make my home, the border between reality and fantasy is notoriously porous. It occurred to me that a trip abroad might help to put some physical and emotional distance between Judas and me. I considered a visit to Jerusalem, a spiritual pilgrimage made by so many seekers over the centuries. Perhaps Judas might finally reveal himself to me in the narrow streets of the Old City.

But my wife, who was becoming concerned by my odd behavior and persistent air of distraction, was strongly opposed. She had read somewhere about "Jerusalem Syndrome", a kind of religious madness to which overwrought tourists occasionally succumb. I was confident a man with my advanced academic training and well-honed rationality would be immune to hysteria of that sort. But my wife continued to voice her worries, so after some discussion we agreed to instead spend a few months in Singapore. That island nation is of course renowned for its stable social order, so firmly regulated by the government. No biblical specters would be allowed to wander through the amusement parks on Sentosa Island, nor lurk in the shopping malls that flank Orchard Road.

I half expected that Judas might forget about me once I crossed the ocean. However, the email communications continued, and there were occasions during my travels in Southeast Asia when his presence seemed tangible. Oddly, it was only after my return to Los Angeles that I began to feel more at ease. My efforts to uncover a Judas lurking in my life had revealed nothing. No one I knew had shown any signs of leading the kind of duplicitous double life that would be required. If Judas was indeed a stalker, it was of the ghostly sort. I have since made my peace with the fact that his identity will remain a mystery, at least to his executor.

But although I did not encounter a resurrected Judas either at home or abroad, his *Gospel* fragments accumulated. It was apparent that Judas was composing (or at least transmitting) his manuscript with little regard for conventional narrative structure. Indeed, I am unsure whether his cryptic farewell to me—"It is finished"— referred to the writing itself, or simply to the author's ability to continue his communications. However, my best guess is that he considered his work to be essentially complete. Judas seemed to have an affinity for numbers, and in particular the number three (perhaps an allusion to the Christian Trinity). He made considerable use of terza rima, or "third rhyme" (the poetic form made famous by Dante). I suspect it is significant that the final poem, "Benediction", consists of three tercets, and is numbered Chapter 27. (The number 27 is, of course, three raised to the third power.)

From time to time I ventured to suggest some small change of wording (typically a metrical variation), which he usually accepted. I have taken some liberty in re-ordering the chapters to perhaps better reflect their natural flow (adding suitable titles). Of course, I took care not to alter the intended meaning in any significant way. My natural curiosity led me to do some research into sources that might have influenced Judas in writing these poems. For those who may be interested, my notes appear at the end.

Early on, Judas suggested that his new *Gospel* should be subtitled *Revised, with a New Introduction by the Author.* However, I pointed out that such an unwieldy title might detract from the impact of his work. In any case, given the circumstances of his untimely demise, it seems improbable that he would have had the opportunity to write down his account during his first lifetime. I do not doubt, of course, that Judas had vividly imagined what his *Gospel* ought to say, and indeed that in his mind he had composed it long ago. Over the millennia to come he may well revise it further. But for us in our time, this is *The Gospel According to Judas.*

Chapter 1. *Double Cross*

"Take me!" I cried, and in confusion flung
Myself between the rabbi and the rood.
"Here's a fine squirming worm, wants to be hung
Beside his King, ripe to wriggle on wood!
Your Majesty, pass sentence on the traitor!"
My shirt was stained already with His blood
From back wounds carved by His interrogator.
That quiet voice: "Father, forgive them all."
"Your King absolves you—you'll regret it later!"
The soldiers nailed us down. "Now hear him bawl!
Let's save a crossbeam spike—join slave with King,
Right hand under left. Now stand them tall!
That pair of posts will serve."
                They let us swing,
Affixed our feet, then left us, dangling.

Women wailed. His blood and pain coursed through
My veins and nerves as though I had been stabbed by
The Christ Himself; and yet His gaze withdrew
From mine and turned toward the thief. "Rabbi,
My Rabbi, why have you forsaken me?
Though I have sinned (as all men must), have I
Not testified for you?"
                "On Calvary,"
The thief broke in, "We all must hang forsaken."
"Join me today in paradise," said He,
Still facing right. Bereaved, the earth was shaken
As wind-blown dust smothered the afternoon.
"Water...." I was alone—He had been taken.
"And me?" Soldiers trudged to their garrison.
"And me?" Whispered the voice, "It has begun."

Chapter 2. *Lamentation*

My God, my God, why have you forsaken me?
I howl in the darkness, cry through the fevered day.

I, who once stood a man among men, crawl lower than a worm,
Crushed, stripped of all substance, bereft of form.

Torn from my mother's womb I sucked fresh hope from her breasts,
Hope later ravaged, strewn before ravenous beasts—

Ravens tear at my eyes, snarling dogs at my feet.
Praying for death I wait, alone—I wait.

The hand of a friend, smile of a woman, laughter of children
Were given to me, but only so as to be taken.

I labored and built great cities, now all of them lie in ruins.
My soul seeps out like sewage, I stare at my bones.

My ears, plugged against curses, are deaf to any blessing—
I did not choose my coming, much less my going.

Others who ached with thirst drank from the stream of faith;
My bucket stayed wedged in the bottomless well of truth.

Jesus, you drew me aside, spoke words to enlighten me—
My God, why have you forsaken me?

Chapter 3. *Samsara*

The gathering of seeds begins
as bit torrents coalesce
across the infinite sphere
without circumference,
rays hurtling through a lens
aimed at the center: here.

The tug of gravity
at ninety-six thousand feet
gives form to vap'rous dust,
figments agglomerate
to seed a memory
hurled back to earth and thrust

into the nascent brain.
Gliding beneath the clouds
familiar smells of earth
awaken genetic codes—
as desert stirs in a rain
the soul prepares for birth.

Confusion of innocence
is rent by the tree of knowledge;
then as the amnesiac
plucks fruit from under its foliage
he's pricked by experience,
cries out to the world, "I'm back!"

Chapter 4. *Invocation of Names*

Call me Jude, or call me Ishmael,
It's all the same to me. What good's a name
Except to shape a puff of wind? I howl
Mine to the desert, hear it echo, "Shame!"
Choose another, Father, choose it well
This time—that old one smells so foul.

I am not the man I used to be,
I am the man created from that man.
Call me Arjuna, call me Enkidu—
Forge a new life for me, shape me a plan!
Mold me a bow and teach me archery,
Train my eye to aim the arrow true.

Character isolated by a deed
Nailed me as a symbol to a cross,
But I climbed down again, back from the dead
Because I could not die. Like gold from dross
The Self poured down to form a tiny seed
Of what a Judas might become instead.

Father, make my name Ananda, ready
To be chosen by the Chosen One.
I will wade into the Jordan's stream
To wash away the life that came undone,
And drown my memories inside an eddy
Until what's past is just a passing dream.

Chapter 5. *Word*

One Word for the wise—
though everything dies
and life feeds on life
by tooth and knife,
though man beats down man
since Cain raised his hand
the unchanging dove
knows God is Love.

OM *shanti shanti shanti*

Chapter 6. *Seed*

Judas, I judge you not
Until I plumb your heart
And grasp your deep desire
For that is who you are,
The seed that starts it all:
Desire becomes your will,
Your will becomes your deed,
Your deed your destiny.

OM *shanti shanti shanti*

Chapter 7. *Return of the Fisher King*

Death is not death that spares such memories.
Coming of age I sensed the vague unease
That creeps upon a mother numb from sleep
    Just before she starts to weep
Remembering her firstborn son has drowned
        Because she turned to save
        His castle from the wave
That drew her boy beneath without a sound.

The trailing clouds of glory turned to slime,
Fouling me with the acrid stench of time.
I changed my name and traveled in disguise
    To join those cheering my demise,
Hanged and stoned and burned and blown apart.
        Hearing in God's cathedral
        How I was turned to evil
I slunk away to wait for some new start.

The lingering shadow of a wounded king
Shimmered as a murder of crows took wing;
I cast my line from off the riverbank,
    Watching as the fish hook sank
Deep in the muddy stream that flows on by.
        What creatures swim below
        I may not ever know
But on the water moves a long-legged fly.

Was not the eye that watched you soothe the gale
The self-same Eye that saw my face turn pale?
Come back, come back, my forlorn soul's companion,
    And lead me once again to Zion!
For if I greatly failed, I greatly dared,
        Remaining your apostle
        Still charged to preach the gospel
So those with ears to hear may yet be spared.

Chapter 8. *Top Ten of Infamy*

Surfing the Internet today I hit
Upon a top-ten list of evil men
Through history. I checked the names on it,
Fearing I'd find my own. Idi Amin
And Vlad Dracul rub shoulders there with Hitler;
Two spots reflect the glory that was Rome—
Caligula, teamed with Nero the fiddler.
Attila the Hun—he looks right at home.
Ivan the Terrible and Joseph Stalin
Made Russia quake; Pol Pot's got hell to pay.
Tomás de Torquemada, holy Christian,
Surely deserves his own *auto-da-fé*.

"Top tens" are always slightly arbitrary—
King Leopold might well have made the list.
How many men did Alexander bury?
Genghis Khan and Mao were somehow missed.
Pope Urban II started the Crusades,
Jerusalem of course the best excuse;
The massacres by Christians on those raids
Helped reconcile the Muslims with the Jews.
And Judas? I don't really fit the bill—
My deed was too allusive, far outdone
By those who relished multitudes to kill.
I never slew a man (worst case, just One).

Chapter 9. *Genesis*

"He's here!" my little servant calls, eyes wide,
"Asking to speak with you!"
                              "Who is it, boy?"
"The healing rabbi." I stand mystified.

I've heard the rumors—crowds aswoon with joy
Hailing their new messiah, cripples leaping,
The blind rejoicing—tricks the hoi polloi

Forever fall for. Charlatans keep creeping
Out of the desert, crying, "I'm a prophet!"
Town to town—healing, stealing, weeping

Like Jeremiah. Now, one more to scoff at?
I am no one's follower—what draws
This rogue to me? The jingle in my pocket?

"Tell him 'Begone'!" I start to say, but pause,
Caught by the awe exuding from the youngster.
The door's ajar; pushing it wide I cross

The threshold.
                    Life—my life—was cut asunder.
Let me start my story over again.
In the beginning—this I still remember:

"A rich man's house was rumored to contain
An empty room, locked tight, the key gone missing;
For many years he searched for it in vain.

The other rooms were furnished, lacking nothing,
And yet the man felt emptiness inside.
He traveled far, seeking out some blessing

He could not name. Returning to abide
In his own home, he found dust and decay
In each neglected room. Dissatisfied,

He gathered the furnishings and gave away
All that he had, until his house stood empty.
And there it lay—the key long gone astray.

The door swung wide, he passed beyond the entry.
Lacking all walls, the room was limitless,
An endless sphere of love, and joy, and plenty."

But that came later—sorry, I digress....
Stepping into my courtyard, I was blinded
By light that coalesced as form and flesh.

One step—his shadow fit me. We were kindred
Sharing a cloak. "Judas Iscariot"
(His voice bespoke a kiss, my name rang sacred),

"You are that son of David, are you not,
Versed in the teachings of Pythagoras?"
I hesitated, then replied, "God taught

Them both to hear the chords rippling across
The heavens; to the Greek He also gave
Numbers to measure what's harmonious

To ear and eye, and showed how numbers wove
Those forms that stood before the earth and stars."
"How great, then, is the measure of God's love?"

"Rabbi, His love is greater than the spheres."
"Lift up your staff, and in your courtyard's dust
Draw the first form relating God to man."

Nodding, I carved a simple line that crossed
Between the two of us. Taking my staff,
The rabbi said, "There is a path that must

Pierce through your barrier," and with a laugh
He drew a line from him to me. "And so
It is that God has cut your life in half."

I stared into the cross as vertigo
Swept over me. He marked a circle round,
Just as a dust devil began to blow.

The cross rose up and spun; it wound
Itself into a sphere, with surface blurred
So that the form embraced us without bound.

Ready to faint, I closed my eyes. I heard
His voice: "Look, there's a fig tree—let us eat
Some fruit and talk awhile, sharing the Word."

And so it was that Jesus came to meet
His Judas. Even now the figs taste sweet.

Chapter 10. *Beatitudes*

For those who wander
without a habitation
   I place the fixed stars
to mark your destination;

For those who hunger
and thirst, unsatisfied,
   my banquet awaits
all guests who step inside.

To those left weeping
alone in desolation
   I come with a smile
to join your celebration;

To lions who walk
among the lambs in peace
   I send forth a child
so love and joy increase.

Chapter 11. *A Sea Crossing*

In memory I hold a mustard seed
And all that from it grew. A crowd had gathered
Early beside the lake. We spoke to plead

For calm, fearing high hopes could turn to hazard
When Jesus came. Peter and Andrew lived
In town; they kept the throng subdued, and measured

Off a small space for him. Jesus arrived
With James and John, and then all twelve of us
Worked hard to keep control as he received

The supplicants. The first the crowd let pass
Fell to his knees and cried out, "Rabbi, heal me—
My arm is paralyzed!"
        "Do you confess

Your sin?"
        "Enraged, I struck my brother—tell me
What I should do."
        "Rise up, you are forgiven
By God and by your brother—go, be healthy."

And so they came—lunatics, cripples, even
A leper, each to place a burden on
The shoulders of the healing rabbi, driven

By pain and drawn by faith. Those who men shun
The rabbi clasped and comforted. Mid-morning
The crowd fell silent, giving way to one

Whose presence signaled danger. Without warning
A Roman soldier stood before us—not
Just some infantryman, but one high ranking,

A tall centurion. He too now sought
Out Jesus—not to seize him, but to seek
His succor. "Lord, my faithful servant caught

A fever; now he lies near death, too weak
To eat or drink. For him I beg your mercy."
"Shall I now follow to your house and speak

With him?"
          "Rabbi, my dwelling is not worthy
That you should enter in. But say a word
And he is cured; I will no longer worry.

I have authority; my voice is heard
And men obey. I tell a soldier, "Go!"
And he will go; "Die!" and he draws sword

And charges though outnumbered by the foe.
Your God has granted you authority
Far greater still."
          "That Israel would show

Such faith as this man does! Go home, for he
Who serves you well is waiting for you there."
Then Jesus left us; shortly we could see

Him kneeling on a hillside, deep in prayer,
As was his custom when the strain of healing
Had worn him down. We needed to prepare

A place for his return, as crowds were swelling
More as the day progressed. The promenade
Was packed along the Galilee, compelling

Jesus to stand on Peter's boat, which made
A pulpit at the water's edge. "Suppose
Your son asks you for bread, would you instead

Give him a stone? And if he asked for clothes
Would you just leave him naked? Ask, and you
Will find that God is generous with those

Who call on Him! But you must not pursue
The treasures of the world, which moths and rust
Corrupt and thieves despoil, but seek the true

Treasure of heaven, worthy of your trust—
For where your treasure lies, there dwells your heart.
Behold a mustard seed! The farmer must

Sow it in fertile soil and help it start
To first take root; but soon the bush stands high
Above the garden, home to birds that dart

Among its branches. Faith will multiply
The seeds that have been planted in your soul—
Go home in peace, for God has heard your cry!"

Shadows grew long, and soon the night would fall.
Our boat set sail; we left Capernaum
To cross the Sea of Galilee. We all

Were more than tired; the rabbi, overcome
By weariness, quickly fell fast asleep.
A squall blew up—clouds turned the sky to gloom,

Whitecaps grew bold, and waves began to leap
Over the gunnels. Peter took the rudder
While Andrew reefed the sails, but still the deep

Rose up against our skiff, sending a shudder
Through wood and sail and ropes and down our spines.
The boat was listing; one more wave might flood her.

Yet Jesus slept, as if we had lifelines
To hold us safe. A gust spun us broadside
As Peter dropped the rudder. All the signs

Showed we were lost, and yet although we tried
To rouse the rabbi, he was in a trance.
I crawled across, and shaking him I cried,

"Teacher, we perish—while there's still a chance
Save us and save yourself!" Then Jesus rose
And laughed at us: "You need deliverance

From ocean spray, and fear a breeze that blows
Us home? You think my Father sent me here
To sleep and drown? Your childish panic shows

Your lack of faith. So be it—I will steer."
He grabbed the rudder, caught a glancing wave
That turned the boat to leeward, helped it veer

Back on our course. "Now hoist the sail, we'll save
Some time by running with the wind." That night
We walked alone along the lake. "You're brave

Indeed, dear Judas—waking me was right."
I could not answer, blushing with delight.

Chapter 12. *Go!*

The seed that sprouts in darkness seeks the light,
The spring that feeds the river finds the sea,
And Word that first was whispered in the night
Shall now be broadcast from the balcony—
Go! Let each apostle act for me,
Healing the flesh and spirit of the weak—
To those with ears to hear, draw close and speak.

Beware of men! Aim to be wise as serpents,
Harmless as doves. Seek out the worthy yet
Be ever vigilant for signs and portents—
Many will mark you as a mortal threat
To their soft clothes and silver. Never let
The roar of power drown an infant's cries—
Harken to newborn babes, they too are wise.

I send you forth as sheep among the wolves,
As empty vessels fit to hold fine wine,
For such are they the Son of Man absolves;
Yet, such are they whom priest and prince consign
To trial—hearing your voices, fearing mine.
Peace to the world? No, I bring a sword
Raised when an open palm exalts the Word!

Father turned against son, son against father—
The sword I wield has cleft your life in twain.
Your neighbors cry, "Our friend's become some other!"
Hated for my sake, what's there to gain?
What gift does rain bestow upon the grain?
That life you've lost, that life is what you're winning—
To know your end, seek first your true beginning.

Chapter 13.

Songs of Mariam Magdala: Wisdom

Wisdom cries from her tower, cries from the high places
       and at the temple gate—
You who enter the deep forest by your own path
       will hear her voice and be glad!
For the Lord possessed me in the beginning of his way
       before his works of old,
Before the earth was formed and the mountains raised
       and the oceans filled.
Even before the void brought forth time and substance
       we lay in the bridal chamber,
And I delighted him through all of that long silence
       preceding the great thunder.
I who am everlasting stayed by his side
       as he set the heavens' compass
And shone the first light upon the worlds he made.
       Hear me! From first to last
I have loved those byways of the universe
       where stand homes and habitations,
Have loved those creatures crawling on scattered spheres—
       mere bits of dust—creation's
Own eyes and ears, each with a world within
       as vast as the world without.
I cry within you, cry out to the sons of men—
       hear what the Lord has wrought!

Chapter 14.
Songs of Mariam Magdala: Lovesick

Asleep at midnight, my heart is wide awake—
    beloved, I hear your knock!
He calls! "Beloved, my sister, my bride, open
    your garden and let me pick
Your orchard fruit, drink from your fountain flowing
    with honeyed milk and with nectar—
Already the night dew gathers upon my locks,
    bring me inside your shelter!"
Lying in bed the door is just out of reach—
    my garments are off, beloved—
My feet have been bathed, how could I rise and soil them,
    how stand before you naked?
Hearing him try the latch, I rise from bed
    and dip my fingers in myrrh;
In haste I reach for my gown, and drawing it on
    at once unbolt the door.
But oh! He has turned and gone into the night,
    gone, and my soul fails me.
My cry, "Beloved, my door has opened for you!"
    brings silence—nothing avails me—
The cobblestones are cold beneath my feet
    and no answer comes.
The watchmen find me searching through the city's
    streets and catacombs;
They beat me, bruise me, rip away my veil,
    these watchmen of the walls.
I beseech you, daughters of Jerusalem,
    make him hear your calls!
Cry out, my sisters! Cast judgment as you will—
    approve or disapprove—
But seek my beloved! And when you find him tell him
    I am sick with love.

Chapter 15.

Songs of Mariam Magdala: Healing

Nothing that enters the body
    defiles the soul,
But poisons spewed from the heart
    desecrate all.

Anointing me with your spittle
    heals my soul,
And naming my demons Legion
    makes me whole.

Chapter 16.

Songs of Mariam Magdala: Love

Your name is an ointment poured upon my soul,
    myrrh rubbed upon my skin;
A hidden garden is my sister, my bride,
    where figs and red grapes ripen.

Beloved, that you were like a brother to me
    who nursed at my mother's breast!
Then I would kiss you, my love, and none despise me,
    none could call me unchaste.

I am yours, beloved, until the shadows flee
    and the song of the dove resounds;
Tonight my love is mine, and I am his,
    and I will heal his wounds.

Our hearts are sealed, for love is strong as death,
    jealousy fierce as the grave;
Love burns as a fire that oceans cannot quench—
    the flame of the Lord is love.

There is no love that is not freely given,
    for love does not speak lies—
That man who for love offers all of his wealth
    we utterly despise.

Chapter 17. *Ocean*

after Mansur al-Hallaj

Born to the earth, I made my way
Back to the ocean whence I came,
Drawn as the moth that seeks the flame,
And fought the waves by night and day.

I punched the breakers—they struck me,
Left me half-broken on the sand,
Until the ocean lent a hand,
Lifted me up and set me free.

And now I do not cease to swim
Buoyed up sometimes on waves of love,
At times pressed under waves above,
While beacons on the shore grow dim.

Chapter 18. *The Road Home*

Spring brought no respite. Always on the move—
Who were we anyway? The chosen army
Of God, pilgrims or vagabonds? Cut loose

Three years from home and family, our journey
Confused us just as much as it enthralled us.
Dodging from soldiers, short on food and money,

We traveled even when the days were coldest,
Pausing where strangers took us in as guests.
One time, out on the road, the rabbi told us,

"Foxes have dens, birds of the air their nests,
And yet the Son of Man has nowhere he
Can lay his head." I thought, all that exists

Can fit inside this man, and yet I see
Into existence this man cannot fit;
Beyond this fleeting world Jesus is free,

Utterly free, but cannot live in it.
How could we not love him? "Lo, the Kingdom
Of God is within—you!" Yes, but the light

That let us see what had been hidden shone from
Him, only him! He healed us, made us healers,
Showed us that love is truth, that love is wisdom.

And that was his undoing. Loving failures,
Sinners and supplicants is dangerous—
Among those seekers, some might well be traitors

Ready to offer Herod Antipas
His reborn John the Baptist! Jesus knew
The risks he ran, but sometimes seemed to miss

The risks we shared—the first time, Herod slew
Just John; he would not be so lax again.
Most followed Jesus blindly, but a few

Of us knew something of the world of men.
Consider how a miracle that feeds
A multitude with bread and fish starts when

Some silver coins are passed around as seeds
Of charity! The shepherd tends his flock—
Blessed are they that tend the shepherd's needs.

All manner sought him out—the lame to walk,
The blind to see, the dead to claw back life.
One time, trapped in a house, I tried to lock

The door—but then the mob ripped off the roof!
Down came a cripple, lowered in a sling,
Crying to Jesus, "Heal me, salve my grief!"

Amazed, we all fell back, forming a ring.
But Jesus kissed him—"Son, you are forgiven."
The man stood up, began to dance and sing.

And so it went—anything could happen—
Lepers would throw themselves down at his feet,
Lunatics would beg his mercy for Satan.

And Lazarus! Jesus went wild, he beat
His chest and raged as though wrestling with God.
When Lazarus ripped off his winding sheet

Jesus had won. Soon after, on the road
South to Jerusalem, I sensed that he
Had changed. The man we loved, who led us, stood

Apart and said, "The world will not see me
After a little while, for now my Father calls
Me home." I answered, "Rabbi, let us see

The Father too."
                        "Judas, would you speak false
As though you never knew me? Hold my face
And gaze into my Father's eyes—no walls

Keep you from Him, nor bar you from the place
I shall prepare for you." He drew me near
With both his hands. I stared into a space

Where my own image floated in a sphere
With no circumference. A shock of vertigo
Came over me, and I drew back in fear.

"I'm hungry," Jesus said, and turned as though
To walk toward a fig tree. I ran first
To pick some fruit for him, but every bough

Was bare. "The tree that promised most proved worst,"
He cried, "and shall forever hence be cursed!"

Chapter 19. *The Golden Gate*

I stood again before the Golden Gate
But found that it was closed to such as me.
Above, the watchmen pelted me with stones
And cried, "Crawl back inside your memory!"
I mocked them, calling, "Those you thought were great
Are heaped together as a pile of bones—
Listen! You can hear their heartsick moans
Below the Temple Mount, now desolate;
But I have heard the promise of the tree
Blasted by wars and shaken at the root
Now back in leaf, portending summer's fruit."

Chapter 20. *Climbing Mount Zion*

The quest to take Jerusalem began
Towards Passover. Jesus rode a donkey
Through the east gate, greeted as the man

Who would be King of Israel—if only
The donkey were a steed, and we had carried
Swords instead of staffs! I was the one he

Would sometimes listen to, and now I worried—
Spring came too soon, the time did not seem right.
He told us little, plans were never solid.

Some wanted him to fight—he would not fight.
Some wanted him to live—he would not live.
But still we followed him, loved him despite

Our apprehensions. He made us believe—
How could we not? "Hosanna!" pilgrims cried,
"Savior of Lazarus, Messiah, give

Your blessing!" Lifted high as on a tide,
Palm branches waving in a swirling sea
Of awestruck faces, his triumphal ride

Swept on up to the temple. Suddenly
I realized the world might just explode—
He, the holiest man, who could well be

The Son of God, climbing to God's abode!
I thought that he would pray—instead, he froze,
Surveying the bazaar, then boldly strode

Into the Court of Gentiles, dealing blows
To moneychangers, setting free the doves.
He raged, "This is the place my Father chose

To build His house of prayer, but what He loves
You've made a den of thieves—clear out, you swine!"
Our hotheads stormed the stalls; curses and shoves

Quickly became a brawl. But at a sign
From Jesus all of us dispersed among
The crowd of pilgrims. Children stood in line

And sang to him, "Hosanna to the Son
Of David!" Jesus hugged them as he mocked
The priests who stood by frowning: "Every one

Of these who sit upon my knee is rocked
Within God's cradle, while you holy knaves
Are cast aside." Hearing him, I was shocked

And fearful—could it be that he who saves
The world might throw away his life, and ours?
For Caiaphas could send us to our graves

For rioting inside his temple—worse,
For blasphemy. I spoke to Jesus as
We made our way to Bethany. "The course

We're on has no good end. If Antipas
Can't catch us, Caiaphas will move instead.
But Rabbi, I have heard the High Priest has

A scholar's mind. No doubt he's been misled
By stories from the scribes—if you could speak
With him alone, perhaps share wine and bread,

You'd make him understand you do not seek
His robes, but only wish to purify
Our offerings to God."
                                   "Another week

And I will make my offering, so why
Would I feed pearls to swine, or care if curs
Lick their own vomit?" Stung by his reply

I said no more. That night was even worse.
Dining with Lazarus became a scene
When Mariam arrived, those eyes of hers

Locking at once with his—the Magdalene,
The Nazarene, adoring and adored!
She pressed an alabaster jar between

Her palms and broke its neck right open, poured
Spikenard upon his head and then his feet;
Weeping, she stroked his skin and called him "Lord".

She shook her long hair loose, and Jesus let
Her wipe his feet with it. Pure nard! The silver
It must have cost would feed five thousand, yet

Jesus did not demur. Seeing me quiver,
He clasped her in his arms and said, "The poor
Will stay with you when I rejoin my Father—

The hour has come to make my body pure,
But only one whose love runs deep can know
What needs be done." Hearing him, I was sure

My teacher, brother, friend was bound for woe,
Slipping away from us. Should I do nothing?
Just listen, watch, keep silent, let him go?

Sometimes a thoughtful man must act, trusting
In God, or instinct. Inquiries were passed
Along, a meeting set. They gave me something

To feed the poor—much less than what we lost
When Mariam despaired, but thirty pieces
Of silver surely helps. My dice were cast.

Hope was reborn, for I had faith in Jesus,
Subtle beyond all men—rendering unto
Caesar his own, so Caesar would not seize us!

Nor Caiphas—for Jesus did not plan to
Overthrow him, just ignore him. Why
Should not the rabbi preach the Word, live on to

Grow old, an honored sage—why must he die?
We twelve dined one last time with him. His face
Was radiant. As though to say goodbye

He came to each of us, eyes full of grace,
And kneeling washed our feet, leaving us stunned.
Jesus declared, "Remember my embrace

In years to come, and this, my one command:
"Love one another!" Giving thanks to God
He passed us bread and wine. He gazed beyond

Us all, and for himself did not take food.
"I am the bread of life, broken for you;
The wine of solace flows as my own blood.

In this, remember me." Then Jesus drew
Me close and whispered, "Kill me, faithful friend—
Now is the time to do what you must do."

I staggered out, confused that he would send
Me off this way—did he condemn, condone,
Command? But I would see it to the end.

At the appointed hour I went alone
To meet the High Priest's men. To my surprise
Soldiers of Rome were there—I had not known

Pilate and Caiaphas were now allies.
The troops marched off with me—no turning back.
Gethsemane—the moon was on the rise.

They all were there—my soul began to quake.
"Who do you seek?"
                              "Jesus of Nazareth."
"I am the one. Judas, do you forsake

The Son of Man?" I kissed him, felt his breath
Against my cheek, and passed him on to death.

Chapter 21. *On the Fig Tree*

Time, time, time, put an end
To me! For I am drained of joy and tears,
Bereft, fruitless as this barren tree
Where I disturb the crows. Oh, let me rend
My cloak and make a noose! What's this I see?
He comes again—the rabbi's face appears,
Eyes abrim with sorrow, scorn and love—
Oh, that I had not been born—stay back!
Clasping my hands, I slip off from the bough.
The pain deep in my guts begins to move.
Within this tunnel looms a monstrous crow—
Fierce white eyes, a blast of wings, then black.

Chapter 22. *Coulda Binna Buddha*

Tried to get some answers
Outa fancy dancers
Listened to a rapper
Rhyme was a disaster
Dude was just a con man
Heh, ya picked the wrong man
Heard a politician
Talkin' 'bout the nation
Everything is outa whack
Time to take the country back
I just hollered, "'Scuse me
Ya done yer best to lose me"
Gotta be a betta way
Lookin' fer a getaway

Binna fool, ditched school
Ran across the Golden Rule
Surfin' on the Internet
Jesus is the best yet
Looked ya up on Facebook
Verses from the praise book
"Heads up fer cheaters
Don't follow leaders
Feed the parkin' meters
Silver change that's Caesar's"
Be meek, be poor
One thing I learnt fershur
Let 'em call us riff raff
We get the last laugh

Heard a brand new gospel
From Judas yer apostle
Claims ya was a hothead
Too soon dead, instead
Shoulda minded Yehuda
Coulda binna buddha
I sez to Judas, "Listen
There's somethin' here yer missin'
S'pose the Cross got crossed out
Guy like me'd be shut out
Ain't settlin' fer a preacher
Lord, I need a reacher
When Jesus died fer sinners
He made us losers winners"

Chapter 23. *Judas Unmasked*

Perhaps I was
the blight that killed the Rose,
    a stain across
the countenance of God—

Or did I make
the perfect sacrifice,
    stab my own soul
so that the Lamb's blood flowed;

Or was I just
a small embellishment,
    picked out to play
an extra in a crowd?

I was perhaps
a splash of ocean foam,
    a drifting leaf,
a clump of broken sod.

Chapter 24. *The Ruined Temple*

My soul is a ruined temple, held fast
By tree roots thrust down through generations
Gone to dust, this serpent tree that fashions
Shackles binding my heart to you, long lost.
I dare not close my eyes for fear I'll miss
Your chariot (as was foretold) descending
From the heavens, the splendor of you standing
Here at the altar of my emptiness.

But no one passes by except a beggar
Scavenging fallen figs along the stream.
At dusk a mockingbird alights and pours
Its song of heartache from this outstretched limb;
Now, as night unfolds, the hands of the Father
Stir the leaves, and sow the sky with stars.

Chapter 25. *Angkor Thom*

I

This is the season of red dust and mangoes.
The memory of rain pulses inside
Moss staining bodhisattvas, inside tangles
Of vines that finger sandstone walls and glide
Through cracks, green fusing with red. The sun goes
On up, relentless. Even lizards hide—
They pay no mind to one old man who's come
To climb the temple steps at Angkor Thom.

The Bayon points the way to Mount Meru
But I am floating on a balsa raft
Along the Ucayali in Peru—
So young then, you and I! We talked and laughed
Like Tom and Huck, life and the world were new,
Caimans on sandbars, red macaws aloft—
Time yet for new friends, though my deadline nears,
But not another friend of fifty years.

I call to mind companions of the river,
Lovers and friends, old rivals too, who shared
The stream with me, for all of us together
Fashioned each other's lives, loved and despaired
Through youth and age. In memory I gather
Also the honored dead, they who prepared
The way with wisdom—rise, those I recall,
That Lokesvara's smile may grace us all!

Lives are floating in time, frozen on walls—
Here ship-borne warriors clash on a lake,
A crocodile devours this one who falls;
Cooks prepare a banquet, gamblers make
Their bets on fighting cocks, a newborn bawls,
A man picks lice from his friend's hair—I take
A backwards step, and though I came alone
Now feel a presence in these halls of stone.

II

Crossing the Terrace of the Leper King
Reminds me of my own disfigurement;
I played a part that cost me everything
Yet never saw the play. Betrayal lent
An extra touch of pathos—his lifespring
Of sacred blood flowed out of friendship rent.
I played the Judas, yes, and bore the loss—
The villain would have kept him from the Cross.

Friend of my trembling soul, if I should meet
You now would twenty centuries have dulled
The pain? If I could kneel before you, beat
My chest and cry, "Forgive me!" would you fold
Your arms around me, lift me up and greet
Me like that lost, prodigal son? You told
Us not to let the sun go down on wrath,
But could it rise with me back on your path?

That barren fruit tree rotted long ago—
Here, this strangler fig soars to the sky,
Spreading to soothe the sun, while down below
Its roots, exposed like holy serpents, try
To meld with temple stone—see how the flow
Of life binds earth with heaven! Tell me, why
Have I crossed oceans seeking out this place?
Is this the tree of knowledge, or of grace?

O bodhisattvas, multi-facetted
As mountain peaks at dawn, gazing within
On silence rising from the fountainhead,
You who have helped the generations spin
Through birth and death, letting compassion spread
To every living being, every sin,
Smile yet on those of us who seek release,
Until our hungering and striving cease!

Chapter 26. *Dialogue of Judas & Jesus*

Judas: Is it strange
   to be the Son of Man?
Jesus: Is it not strange
   to be anything at all?

Judas: What is it like to become a man?
Jesus: To suffer a grievous blow,
   regaining consciousness to find
   oneself diminished,
   memories
   just out of reach,
   words jostling one another
   to form a crude sequential artifact.

Judas: What is unknowable by One
   Who is omniscient?
Jesus: The pangs of doubt and confusion.

Judas: What capacity of the human mind
   eludes the power of One
   both omniscient and omnipotent?
Jesus: The gift of self-deception.

Judas: What capacities of the human mind
   open our hearts to the infinite?
Jesus: To find truth in numbers,
   to feel the lifeblood
   pulsing through a poem.

Judas: Why did you choose
        this time and place and people?
Jesus: Such obstinate folk—
        laboring beneath the imperial yoke
        still they reap fierce delight
        disputing among themselves
        what God intends for them—
        who could resist their charm?

Judas: Why would Jesus love
        one so unworthy as I?
Jesus: I, the Only Son,
        never knew a brother's love.

Judas: Why me,
        more than our brother Peter?
Jesus: In my time of trial Peter denies me;
        but in full view of my mortal enemies
        Judas greets me with a kiss.

Judas: How is it, at the end?
Jesus: Dying a man, I feel a man's regrets—
        Not for the sacrifice, the great work done
        For which I lived, knowing my death completes
        My Father's pledge, the duty of His Son,

        But I will miss the lesser, human joys—
        Laughter of children, sea foam, cries of birds,
        The taste of figs, and she with kohl-dark eyes
        Who heard my voice beyond the sound of words.

Chapter 27. *Benediction*

Do not grieve overlong when I am gone,
Fearing that I have left you here alone.
The time for weeping ends; let tears be done.

Bow to the four directions—I am there.
I guide the sun, the moon, the morning star,
And catch the swallow falling from the air.

I am with you always, in the bead
Of dew upon the lotus, in the reed
Beside the lake, and in the mustard seed.

EXECUTOR'S NOTES

Setting aside the mystery surrounding the identity of the resurrected Judas, there remains the more amorphous mystery of his literary sources. I am neither a scholar of religions nor a theologian, so make no pretense of fully grasping his mash-up of allusions. Still, my curiosity was piqued. Taking my cue from the exemplary scholarship of Jorge Luis Borges (author of the essay "Three Versions of Judas"), I made an effort to trace apparent influences. These notes summarize some connections I believe I have discovered. These remain conjectures, and doubtless some important sources have been missed.

Many passages and incidents in Judas' writings resonate with passages from Judeo-Christian scripture. These sources include the canonical gospels and Gnostic texts, as well as chapters from the Old Testament. For example, the "Songs of Mariam Magdala" appear to be based on Proverbs 8 ("Wisdom") and Song of Solomon ("Lovesick", "Love"). Biblical scholars will doubtless be able to identify other specific parallels, but as an amateur I was not up to the task of investigating all the possible cross-references. Perhaps more surprisingly, I detected apparent influences of the eastern religions, Hinduism and Buddhism (especially "Samsara", "Word", "Seed" and "Angkor Thom"). Also, a few poems seem to contain echoes of passages from mystical Sufi poets. The most notable of these is Mansur al-Hallaj, whose proclamations of oneness with God in the 10th century gave his enemies an excuse to subject him to a martyrdom even more horrific than that experienced by Jesus. Judas acknowledges al-Hallaj in "Ocean", a poem adapted from a passage in which the Sufi describes the "sea of love". A line from a Persian ghazal found its way into "Lamentation" (a poem apparently based largely on Psalm 22).

As might be expected given the affinity with Yeats that marked our early email correspondence, several of Judas' poems seem to owe him debts—for example, a borrowed line in "Invocation of Names", and the stanza form of "Return of the Fisher King" (the same as that of Yeats' "Byzantium"). Another 20th-century poet, T. S. Eliot, also appears to have been an influence. In particular, the motif of the "fisher king", which originated in Arthurian legend, was famously used by Eliot in "The Wasteland".

Let me briefly mention a few other details I was able to discover that relate to specific poems.

Double Cross

Traditionally, it has been said that a common criminal was crucified on each side of Jesus. The Bad Thief (on the left) mocked Jesus; the Good Thief (on the right) rebuked the mocker, and was granted a place in the Kingdom of God. It seems Judas claims (or imagines) that it was he who was crucified to the left of Jesus, with whom he shared a single crossbeam, while a single thief was on the right.

Samsara

In eastern religions, samsara refers to the cycle of birth, death and rebirth. The phrase "infinite sphere without circumference" derives from a quote from the mathematician and Christian philosopher Blaise Pascal (also attributed to earlier sources).

Invocation of Names

I was able to discover plausible sources for all of the names introduced in this poem, which perhaps alludes to the plea, "Father, change my name," from Leonard Cohen's song "Lover Lover Lover". Jude is a variant (more popular in contemporary usage) of Judas. "Call me Ishmael" is the famous first sentence of Melville's *Moby Dick*. In the Old Testament, Ishmael was the first son of Abraham by his wife's handmaiden, later displaced in his father's affection by his half-brother Isaac (Abraham's son by his wife). In the *Bhagavad Gita*, Arjuna is a fabled warrior (an archer without peer) who listens to and accepts the teachings of the divine Krishna. Enkidu was the warrior companion of the great king Gilgamesh in the ancient Mesopotamian poem of that name. Enkidu's death (killed as a punishment for offending the gods) and Gilgamesh's extravagant grief form a pivotal episode of the story. Ananda was a faithful disciple and companion of the Buddha. The Self alludes to the concept of Atman in Hindu philosophy, a person's divine essence or soul.

The Return of the Fisher King

In various places and times, an effigy of Judas has been burned or otherwise abused in a festival preceding Easter Sunday ("the Burning of Judas"). The "eye" in the final stanza may be derived from a sermon by Meister Eckhart, a medieval Christian mystic, where he says, "The eye with which I see God is the same with which God sees me."

Top Ten of Infamy

Since not all of the names listed are widely known today, it may be useful to review the cast of villains. Order of mention does not, I believe, imply a ranking.

The Ten: Idi Amin, brutal President of Uganda, 20th century; Vlad III (family name Dracul), Prince of Wallachia, called "the Impaler", 15th century CE; Adolf Hitler, no need for introduction; Caligula and Nero, the two most scandalous Emperors of Rome, 1st century CE; Attila the Hun, plunderer of Europe, 5th century CE; Ivan IV, called "the Terrible", Tsar of All the Russias, 16th century CE; Joseph Stalin, Communist dictator who ruled the Soviet Union by terror, executing hundreds of thousands as "enemies of the people", 20th century; Pol Pot, leader of the Khmer Rouge in Cambodia who oversaw that country's "killing fields", 20th century; Tomás de Torquemada, friar and architect of the Spanish Inquisition, who blended Mass with torture and execution to create the rite of *auto-da-fé* ("act of faith"), 15th century CE.

The Dishonorable Mentions: King Leopold II of Belgium, instigator of horrific atrocities inflicted on the native people of the Belgian-ruled Congo, late 19th - early 20th century; Alexander III of Macedon, called "the Great", conqueror of lands from the Ionian Sea to the Himalayas, who imported the cultural practice of crucifixion from Persia to Greece (later passed on to Rome), 4th century BCE; Genghis Khan, founder of the Mongol Empire, with a penchant for massacring local populations, late 12th - early 13th century CE; Mao Zedong, founder of the People's Republic of China, responsible for the deaths of millions in wars and famines, 20th century; Pope Urban II, initiator of the First Crusade, later beatified by the Catholic Church, 11th century CE.

Genesis

This account of the earliest meeting between Judas and Jesus is the first of several narrative chapters written in terza rima. David, the great king of Israel, was an acclaimed master of the harp. Pythagoras was a legendary Greek mathematician, philosopher and mystic. He believed that numbers and mathematics provide the basis of reality, that music (itself an expression of mathematical relations) creates the "harmony of the spheres", and that the soul has a continuing existence beyond the material world, with which it has a mystical connection. Pythagorean ideas (some traceable to yet earlier Orphic beliefs) had a direct influence on the philosophy of Plato. Pythagoras founded a secretive society, which became a model for many later esoteric groups, including Gnostic Christianity. Many such groups, as well as other traditions that developed independently of Western civilization, have given symbolic interpretations to combinations of geometric forms. Here, Judas apparently sees a cross within a circle become three-dimensional, and then gyrate into an indefinite sphere (compare "Samsara", 1st stanza). The fig tree may perhaps be associated with the tree of knowledge from the biblical Genesis. It may also have a connection to the story of how Jesus, as he approached Jerusalem, cursed a fig tree that did not bear fruit at a time he was hungry (Mark 11:12-25). The fig tree turns out to be a recurrent motif in Judas' poems.

Go!

The stanzas that Judas uses in telling how Jesus sent forth his apostles are written in rhyme royal.

Songs of Mariam Magdala

Judas refers to Mary Magdalene by her name in Aramaic, their native tongue. Perhaps he simply liked its musicality.

The Golden Gate

The Golden Gate is the name given to the oldest of the current gates in the walls of Jerusalem's Old City, located on the eastern side. Many believe that Jesus entered the city on Palm Sunday through an earlier version of this gate. According to Jewish tradition, this is the entrance that the Messiah will use to enter Jerusalem. Perhaps to prevent this from ever happening, the gate has been sealed since the 16th century CE.

Coulda Binna Buddha

You can imagine my surprise when I received the email from Judas with this chapter (on an Easter Sunday!). Besides the jarring discord between the style and tone of this poem and all the previous ones, it has an odd self referential quality, commenting on (and in some ways undercutting) Judas and his *Gospel*, while being part of it. I have to say I found it rather amusing how the speaker (apparently some poorly-educated punk) ends up dismissing Judas' carefully-reasoned argument that Jesus needed to be saved from himself, instead making a forceful case for the Christian view of Christ the Redeemer of sinners. And yet, is not the speaker also somehow Judas? The poem left me scratching my head.

As for the style, it reminds me of Bob Dylan's classic

song, "Subterranean Homesick Blues". Perhaps as a kind of homage to it, the "verse" quoted in the second stanza seems like a twisted blend of the biblical lines "Beware of false prophets" and "Render unto Caesar that which is Caesar's" with Dylan's "Don't follow leaders / Watch the parkin' meters."

Incidentally, "Yehuda" is the Hebrew equivalent of "Judas". It seems a bit improbable that the uneducated speaker would happen to know this, but I imagine it was hard to come up with any better rhyme for "buddha".

The Ruined Temple

The metaphor in the title can perhaps be better understood in light of the poem that follows it.

Angkor Thom

More than any other, this poem fueled my suspicion that Judas was somehow stalking me. The poem, written in stanzas of ottava rima, is divided into two sections; Judas brazenly made me the voice of the first part, and himself the voice of the second. In the spring of 2014 I did in fact visit the ancient temple complex at Angkor Thom in Cambodia (near the more famous site of Angkor Wat). However, I traveled with my family, not alone as the poem suggests. It is also the case, as suggested in the second stanza, that decades ago I rafted down the Ucayali River (one of the sources of the Amazon)—in 1971 I spent a week on the river with my friend Nick Robinson. I have no explanation for how Judas was able to glean these personal details.

The Cambodian spring follows the end of the wet monsoon season. The weather is dry and hot; red dust (from dissolved sandstone) coats everything, and mangoes turn ripe in the aftermath of the rainy season. The imagery of Angkor Thom, the final capital of the Khmer kingdom (late 12th to 17th centuries), figures prominently in this poem. The temple complex is a unique fusion of Buddhist and Hindu architecture and carvings. The central temple, the Bayon, is shaped to resemble Mount

Meru, a mythical mountain in the cosmology of both religions. The temple's towers feature over two hundred gigantic faces (many appearing as four-faced heads) representing Lokesvara, the bodhisattva of compassion.

After Angkor Thom was abandoned, the site was overgrown by the jungle over the course of many centuries; when it was excavated in the 20th century, some parts of the walls were left in the grip of the roots of large trees. One species of these is the strangler fig (surely a double entendre for Judas, given the role that its Middle Eastern cousin seems to have played in his bitter end). The fourth stanza describes scenes from Khmer life that are carved into friezes on walls. The Terrace of the Leper King takes its name from a statue found at that site, discolored by moss and algae, which according to legend portrays an early Khmer monarch who was afflicted with leprosy (an Eastern echo, perhaps, of the Arthurian fisher king).

Dialogue of Judas and Jesus
The opening calls to mind some blend of the philosopher Thomas Nagel ("What is it Like to Be a Bat?") and the singer/songwriter Jeff Mangum of Neutral Milk Hotel (final line of "In the Aeroplane Over the Sea").

ALSO BY KEITH HOLYOAK

Foreigner: New English Poems in Chinese Old Style
(Dos Madres Press, 2012)

My Minotaur: Selected Poems 1998-2006
(Dos Madres Press, 2010)

Facing the Moon: Poems of Li Bai and Du Fu
bilingual edition of translations from the Chinese
(Oyster River Press, 2007)

Poetry CDs from Broken Electric Records
(www.BrokenElectric.com):
Selections from My Minotaur (2012)
Poems of Du Fu (2009)
Poems of Li Bai (2007)
Keith Holyoak's Descent (2006)

About the Author

Keith Holyoak at Angkor Thom, Cambodia, 2014

Keith Holyoak was raised on a dairy farm in British Columbia, Canada. With degrees in psychology from the University of British Columbia and Stanford University, his scientific work focuses on the nature of human thinking and its basis in the brain. He has been a recipient of a Guggenheim Fellowship, and is a Fellow of the American Association for the Advancement of Science. Currently he is a Distinguished Professor of Psychology at the University of California, Los Angeles.

Mary Margaret Alvarado - *Hey Folly* (2013)

John Anson - *Jose-Maria de Heredia's Les Trophées* (2013),
  Time Pieces - poems & translations (2014)

Jennifer Arin - *Ways We Hold* (2012)

Michael Autrey - *From The Genre Of Silence* (2008)

Paul Bray - *Things Past and Things to Come* (2006),
  Terrible Woods (2008)

Ann Cefola - *Face Painting in the Dark* (2014)

Jon Curley - *New Shadows* (2009), *Angles of Incidents* (2012)

Grace Curtis - *The Shape of a Box* (2014)

Sara Dailey - *Earlier Lives* (2012)

Dennis Daly - *Nightwalking with Nathaniel-poems of Salem* (2014)

Richard Darabaner - *Plaint* (2012)

Deborah Diemont - *Wanderer* (2009), *Diverting Angels* (2012)

Joseph Donahue - *The Copper Scroll* (2007)

Annie Finch - *Home Birth* (2004)

Norman Finkelstein - *An Assembly* (2004), *Scribe* (2009)

Karen George - *Swim Your Way Back* (2014)

Gerry Grubbs - *Still Life* (2005), *Girls in Bright Dresses Dancing* (2010),
  The Hive-a book we read for its honey (2013)

Richard Hague - *Burst, Poems Quickly* (2004),
  During The Recent Extinctions (2012)

Ruth D. Handel - *Tugboat Warrior* (2013)

Pauletta Hansel - *First Person* (2007), *What I Did There* (2011)

Michael Heller - *A Look at the Door with the Hinges Off* (2006),
  Earth and Cave (2006)

Michael Henson - *The Tao of Longing & The Body Geographic* (2010)

R. Nemo Hill - *When Men Bow Down* (2012)

W. Nick Hill - *And We'd Understand Crows Laughing* (2012)

Eric Hoffman - *Life At Braintree* (2008), *The American Eye* (2011),
  By The Hours (2013)

James Hogan - *Rue St. Jacques* (2005)

Keith Holyoak - *My Minotaur* (2010), *Foreigner* (2012)
Nancy Kassell - *Text(isles)* (2013)
David M. Katz - *Claims of Home* (2011), *Stanzas on Oz* (2015)
Sherry Kearns - *Deep Kiss* (2013)
Burt Kimmelman - *There Are Words* (2007),
    The Way We Live (2011)
Jill Kelly Koren - *The Work of the Body* (2015)
Ralph La Charity - *Farewellia a la Aralee* (2014)
Pamela L. Laskin - *Plagiarist* (2012)
Owen Lewis - *Sometimes Full of Daylight* (2013)
Richard Luftig - *Off The Map* (2006)
Austin MacRae - *The Organ Builder* (2012)
Mario Markus - *Chemical Poems-One For Each Element* (2013)
Patricia Monaghan - *Mary-A Life in Verse* (2014)
J. Morris - *The Musician, Approaching Sleep* (2006)
Rick Mullin - *Soutine* (2012), *Coelacanth* (2013),
    Sonnets on the Voyage of the Beagle (2014)
Fred Muratori - *A Civilization* (2014)
Robert Murphy - *Not For You Alone* (2004),
    Life in the Ordovician (2007), *From Behind The Blind* (2013)
Pam O'Brien - *The Answer To Each Is The Same* (2012)
Peter O'Leary - *A Mystical Theology of the Limbic Fissure* (2005)
Bea Opengart - *In The Land* (2011)
David A. Petreman - *Candlelight in Quintero-bilingual ed.* (2011)
Paul Pines - *Reflections in a Smoking Mirror* (2011),
    New Orleans Variations & Paris Ouroboros (2013),
    Fishing on the Pole Star (2014),
    Message from the Memoirist (2015)
Samantha Reiser - *Tomas Simon and Other Poems* (2015)
William Schickel - *What A Woman* (2007)
David Schloss - *Behind the Eyes* (2005)
Don Schofield - *In Lands Imagination Favors* (2014)
Daniel Shapiro - *The Red Handkerchief and other poems* (2014)

Murray Shugars - *Songs My Mother Never Taught Me* (2011),
    Snakebit Kudzu (2013)

Jason Shulman - *What does reward bring you but to bind you to
    Heaven like a slave? (2013)*

Maxine Silverman - *Palimpsest (2014)*

Lianne Spidel & Anne Loveland - *Pairings* (2012),
    Bird in the Hand (2014)

Olivia Stiffler - *Otherwise, we are safe* (2013)

Carole Stone - *Hurt, the Shadow-the Josephine Hopper poems* (2013)

Nathan Swartzendruber - *Opaque Projectionist* (2009)

Jean Syed - *Sonnets* (2009)

Madeline Tiger - *The Atheist's Prayer* (2010),
    From the Viewing Stand (2011)

James Tolan - *Red Walls* (2011)

Brian Volck - *Flesh Becomes Word* (2013)

Henry Weinfield - *The Tears of the Muses* (2005),
    Without Mythologies (2008), *A Wandering Aramaean* (2012)

Donald Wellman - *A North Atlantic Wall* (2010),
    The Cranberry Island Series (2012)

Sarah White - *The Unknowing Muse* (2014)

Anne Whitehouse - *The Refrain* (2012)

Martin Willetts Jr. - *Secrets No One Must Talk About* (2011)

Tyrone Williams - *Futures, Elections* (2004),
    Adventures of Pi (2011)

Kip Zegers - *The Poet of Schools* (2013)

www.dosmadres.com